the slipped leash

for all the Benthams

the slipped leash

PAUL HENRY

seren

Seren is the book imprint of
Poetry Wales Press Ltd
Nolton Street, Bridgend, Wales
www.seren-books.com

The right of Paul Henry to be identified as the
Author of this Work has been asserted in accordance with
the Copyright, Designs and Patents Act, 1988

ISBN 1-85411-323-2

A CIP record for this title is available from the British Library

The publisher acknowledges the financial assistance
of the Arts Council of Wales

Printed in Palatino by Gwasg Dinefwr, Llandybie

Cover photograph by Cassandra Jones, 'Cath and Jasmine'

Contents

I

II

I

"A life can be haunted by what it never was
If that were merely glimpsed ..."

Louis MacNeice – 'Selva Oscura'

The Short Cut to the Sea

No one's charted this way
except by heart. The bay
opens up at the end.

Already stitching the torn land
back to the dazzling sea
or bending to untie
the straps from your brown feet,
you've left me behind.

"Wait for me! Wait!"
cries the land to the sea.

Memento

Audrey's bolt won't save us
though every night I slide it across,
transplant it to new front doors when we move.

The boys can't reach it yet.
It opens and closes their days
and holds time in its frame
when they sleep.

Three clicks; it's a neat act,
like making a rifle safe
and the old girl must have loved it,
locking her tenants out, her loneliness in.

Half asleep, we listen to the rain,
grow old behind glass waterfalls

while downstairs, cocked like a trigger,
the window someone forgot to shut
lets in our ghosts again.

The Slipped Leash

It sways from a branch out the back
and from it hangs a nut cage.

The handstrap still whiffs of him
for all the wind and rain –
sea dog, country dog.

What misfits we'd have made,
haunting this town's streets,
our walks cut into neat
desperate portions of breath.

Now he's free and I stay in

and the nut cage swings
with winter at its wire

and someone else's dog barks.

Of Small Consequence

that the train now standing at platform 4
(Willesden Junction)
has no Edward Thomas on board

*

that the dream ended here
at this bend in the line
this bar's rest in the tune

this skylit room
with its one brown hair
in the pillow's dint

that felt the sun's heat

*

that one thing is like another
and love no longer a question
of how the sun falls
but that however different
the trains we inhabit
it falls on you and me
at precisely the same time
and that we both know it

*

that some work their hopes
to the bone and never earn this light
which is yours and mine

*

that two towns flooded –
the one you grew up in
and the one you became

and that all the water gods agreed
that this was more tears
than even Helen deserved

*

that here is love's no man's land
the disused line where nettles thrive
over half-submerged sleepers

where our ghosts rise
unlock hands
and drift away down diminishing tracks –
one to the east and one to the west –

without looking back

Heredity

I often hear the same car
reversing in another street
like a sliding bow,
a badly played violin.

And always the moon through pylons
is my father behind bars.

Waist deep in his light
I limp across blue fields,
dragging the wound called love
as far as the water's edge,

returning in time
for a door aching wide in the sky

and, played perfectly
by a neighbour's tree

the moon's huge minim

                    set free

A Model Railway

Peering in through windows we see them,
our parents, dimly lit
"for authenticity", reading *Wizard*
or *Girl's Own*... or buying another hotel
on Old Kent Road, speculating
for dreams, between the tracks
and broccoli-like trees.

Or are they the ones in the tunnel,
whose hair he painted white,
who wait in darkness for a signal,
remembering the war?

                A whistle blows.
On a platform, holding their pose,
Trevor Howard and Celia Johnson
won't let go, won't let go

Inside the Walled Garden

Leaning against your evergreen oak
that sense, between a glass
and a bottle, of having screwed up,
of having missed a step
in the dark, as a child,

of tumbling down through branches
and landing in middle age, is fanned
by a cool half-a-million leaves.

Somewhere, behind the original eaves,
your kids and mine play *Monopoly*.
It's the same dice in their hands,
the same closely held secret
suddenly spilled.

             Love's currency
rustles over their heads, its chances
turned and squandered by the wind.

I look at you through my glass.
Time hasn't touched your face.
Beyond, in the vast kitchen,
the flaccid eel on your Corris slate
looks back, philosophical
beneath your husband's knife.

As Close as it Gets

Perhaps if they made love, once
in a cheap hotel
where the shower's broken
and the dead fly on the window sill
won't tell, once
then it would be enough.

It's late August; they meet in the rain.
There's a place off the Rue de Lape
with a mannequin on Reception
and no light in the stairwell.
By the time they reach the room
he's held her that close
it's almost as close as it gets,
closer than wet hair.

Above the bed a boy and girl
stroll through a fishing village
down to a biblical sunset...

The overhead fan stops.
A damp summer's intimacies
begin to turn stale.

A last kiss drops
and there's nothing left to give
and this, surely, perhaps,
is all they came here for,
perhaps,
or perhaps they want more,

to follow the boy and girl above them
all the way down to the shore.

DOM IS A HOM

for Wil T.

We haven't come out to play
for twenty-five years.

Our hair is turning grey
as the sea, the buried slipway.

We dig and clack the pebbles,
old against new, like castanets,

searching for *DOM IS A HOM*,
the wall we warmed our backs on.

Boarded up against the tide
the disused student hall bears down,

howls each night as we run,
laughing like girls, away from Dom,

the studs in our heels clicking still
up the tide's echoing stairwell.

Boys

I need them, to muscle in on this silence,
to measure the softening tissue in my arms
when I carry them up to their beds,
when the old house creaks like a galleon
after a storm.

Set adrift on their dreams
their faces turn soft again.
So that one kiss carries the weight
of all we try to make light of.

Giant Leaps

What chapel lives we might have had!
What parsimonious slices of love!
With Salem over the upright
and *Crist yw pen y tŷ hwn...*
and the century cornered inside our *Bush*.
Its organ-stop buttons alternate
between *Dechrau Canu...* and Apollo 11.
Look! There's Neil (you be Neil)
and here's me, Buzz, upstaged
but glad to be still in the race.
We smack the sofa's arms
and watch the stardust rise,
stress no more than a sermon
to polish when the Lay's away.
What chapel lives! One small step
surely, with such a simple set.
Warm your palm awhile my dear
on this faithless cabinet
and pray for our time as it dies.
Beyond your window's crucifix
Newton, Einstein, Edison
and other village luminaries
are walking their curious frowns
as far as the lane's end.
Small incinerations of thought
rise between the birdsong as they pass.
The graveyard's crooked equations
and pipeman's philosophies
wait, patiently, for a solution.
Don't stare at the sun too long dear.
Take off this prickly shawl.
Ours the black book and kettle,

the standard lamp in the hall,
the blues under the pews
and the laptop under the bed.
What chapel lives we might have led!

Acts

There are months of not loving you
when the plates we keep spinning
simply spin, but today I woke
and broken china surrounded the bed.
Today was loving you again.

I limped into a small garden,
knowing that soon, in spite of us,
the plots of soaps would drone on,
the commentaries from transistors
on allotments, the bees in the fuchsias,
the trains slowing down or gathering speed
with somebody on them thanking Christ
they don't live here, or there...

I have given up trying to piece together
so many broken plates, to perfect
the circus acts of love.

                              I remember
that once, in the sun's spotlight,
our dust made a merry-go-round.
I remember a rippling field
and sand slipping from under our feet.

I remember that much of loving you.

                    *

One shirt, one dress on a line
(such acrobatics – the leaves hold their breath
and then applaud) yours and mine –
the closest we'll come to a fall.

                    *

How is the knife thrower?
Of all the eyes in the audience
he picked out yours. And so it was that,
after he'd made you his squaw,
I watched you turn weak at the knees

and somewhere, beneath all the smiles,
heard the lions roar.

*

There are months of not loving you
when the lion tamer's charm is enough.
She's easily as brown as you
and the jungle in her eyes
matches the ocean in yours.

But when she leaves the cage ajar
an impulse makes for your shore.

*

Today the strongman cracked.
The tributaries in his neck
erupted with lava.
His fixed grin crumbled
and an avalanche of teeth
bit the dust.

When he fell
the whole house shook and the weights
spun off the end of all he'd held dear.

Glancing in the mirror he saw
Saturn without its rings,
Christ without his halo,
the Mona Lisa without her smile,
a universe of ash...

*

There are months of not loving you,
empty domes for the mildly insane,
where The Prozac Clowns rehearse...
'Timing, timing is everything!'
calls Zac to Coco (on his arse
with a blade through his brain).

And there are days, tumbling days
that blur your face,
when the woman spinning by her smile
could be anyone.

But not this day.
I missed you in the lunch-hour crowd,
the pull and push of its currents
beneath my aching feet

and every so often,
through tears in the canopy,
your blue eyes staring back
from another time.

Exmouth

Here's where we dug water for gold
countless revolutions ago

where small men at their wells
wound up the tide as we slept

then let it slip out of sight,
like a sheet the river kicked down

so we'd wake up frozen, afraid of dry land.

There must be one, in a dusty box
at the creaking back of a hardware store

or at the end of a washing line's
anarchic semaphore

still winding
and winding up nothing

but the salt of you and me.

Easter Break

Every day the landlord's spy
pegs another mole on the wire
surrounding our "mountain retreat".
A boy-hating ex-marine
he's booby-trapped the place
with breakables:
fractured plates, cracked toilet seats,
landscapes that fall
when brushed against
and, in the games room,
split snooker cues, warped darts...

The boys are wild.
Handles come off in their paws,
mud gives their hideouts away.
They like to shock each other.
They know, like the wind,
that glass is a lie
waiting to be exposed.
Before I can reach him
the youngest
launches an axe into space.
Pioneers of the wilderness
they won't be trained
by fences or walls.
They know the holiday is short.

When we leave,
like the moles on the barbed wire
they wave
with cute big hands at the spy,
at the field they once explored.

Llangors

When the lake froze
Major Raikes walked on it,
boys threw stones on it,
Prosser prayed on it,
Jean Drew painted it...

and you and I,
after they'd all fallen through
the night's long crack,
just stared at it,
listened to the moonlight creak.

Our boat, set in its grip,
would have done for a bed
but, older than our years,
we knew, or thought we did,
that the moon on the lake was enough.

Slipping on Leaves
for D.

The women behind the ochre screen
weren't trying on your clothes
but slipping on leaves.

Their bearded husbands
nodded when they twirled,
nursed pipes like unhatched eggs.

We heard the backward clocks
go tock-tock-tock...
and felt the cut of the moment.

The market's sky-blue din slurred
like a swimming gala crowd
to a diver cracking the surface

and somewhere near, in a hedgerow
a beak was ticking its way through a shell.

You waved to the wicker man each time
his beer gut snagged against our stall
and when he smashed the woodturner's bowl.

(Glued back, varnished over
 so the fissure hardly showed,
 like love, it still sold).

I took out the ring from my ear and,
prepossessed, slipping on love,
eased it along your finger,

                    pausing
at the widest joint, the hip

before pushing it all the way.

Sheds

A friend opened his, dressed it
in ribbons; speeches were made.
A priest blessed it.

The public queued to get in,
surprised to find nothing inside
but the soul of a shed, a man.

*

The one I inherited fell apart.
Others might have knocked it down.
Too many ghosts to hurt

I watched it decompose –
kennel, bird's nest, (flown),
sanctuary for the breeze...

*

The village halls of Wales squat
and let the rain do its worst,
are sometimes mistaken for toilets.

*

An arch, two pews, a man,
a boy, a flask's chalice –
the putty-wafer communion.

Doorsteps crumble in the mouth.
When the elder smiles
tar burns between his teeth.

*

Sheds

Ah, the ubiquitous writing shed,
sky-blue, the sun on its crest,
its wings lined with lead,

where the raging heart's affairs
were secretly confessed,
hoping someone might hear.

*

The Manicure

Against her own varnished skies
ten sunflowers bloom. Her eyes
are someone he once almost kissed.

She holds his third finger still
like a bride at the altar, then asks
if one layer or two will do.
She's new to cracked guitarists.

So she's never heard of Al Stewart.
So she slips acid into his cut.
So she knows he doesn't know where it's at...
Her laugh's enough.

It leads his heart,
its fat, ugly hand in hers,
back to that field of sunflowers.

Fable

So many lives out there
and one of them is ours.
We lie in late on Sundays
and pitch a tent now and then,
to remember the stars.
Your name is Eve, by the way.
You ride to sleep on my lap.
Aeroplanes gate-crash our dreams.
The daylight discovers us
naked, legs drawn up
in the same, foetal hug.
We're closer than twins
and you are the sensible one.

Here comes the week, the wolf
bearing clichés to our door.
Soon we have three daughters.
I lose my mind, my hair.
I take to wandering moors.
My belly rumbles in greasy bars.

You join a kick-boxing class,
acquire an eye for fast cars.
The girls are in their teens.
You're calm when they turn on us.
We haven't pitched a tent for years
but here is the same sheet
beneath us, and here
above us, the same stars.

Where are you Eve?
We've never needed each other more
now that the girls have flown,
now that we're old and grey,
our pilgrim souls fully-clothed.

How crazy must we become
before we recognise ourselves?
Did we mean to leave it like this:
a moth-eaten tent in the attic
and look, pitched where a slate was,
the much-loved stars?

Loving the Beekeeper

How sweet does it have to be?

Work, drones, work,
from China to Canada,
from Palestine to Peru,

from the flowers in her dress
to the sun's broken jar,
its fragments of dew,

from last summer's hive
to this one's, tuning up
in the loudening blue...

In the name of love,
work, drones, work.

*

Safely back in our cell,
our hotel bellowed by the tide,
I kneel beside the skep,
her punctured bonnet,
the useless husks of underclothes,
an empty jar of baby oil....

She can still hear them
stalking us all the way here.

Chimneys, keyholes...
all entrances are sealed.

Near the Edge

Soon they'll be out of breath –
heads down, too quickly
along the cliff-top path.

Soon they'll have to notice the sea,
how silver and full of promise
it's become, in spite of them.

*

Inside the *Café El Dali*
the dying drink to flamenco
and pick at what they can,

Madonna With Cigarette
rolls her own Passing Cloud
under a fishing net
that lets in the sun.

Behind her, bright fins
make figures of eight
in the bay's aquarium.

Matadors fade on the wall.
The waiter locks the door,
strums an empty chair.

Smoke rises, everywhere.

*

The cliff is not a precipice
but a kiss
about to happen.

When he glances over the edge
and into her eyes
something holds him back

while out on the vague horizon

liners

      shells of the snails
they used to be

          leave trails

quickly covered by the sea.

The Kissing Gate

They have walked through into the other field
more than once,
gripped the lever and let
the bird caged in its rust fly.

Across these bars
their lips introduced each other,
across the dazzling years

for a few seconds, long enough
to finally seal inside
what some call friendship
and others love.

Scrolled eight times in its frame,
to remind him,
her initial, *S... S... S...*
prints itself on the blinding sea.

The Conker Boys

Light fades.
The motorway drowns the river.

The little one stuffs his boots
so that when he walks it's torture.

The tree's time machine
knows these boys of old.

Its torn flags hang still
as street shepherds

who park their dogs on the bank
and stare across

to fields not yet built upon
where the sheep are.

Light fades.

Each thorny case broken into
lets out a "Cor!"

The park keeper blows his whistle.

Hunters, thieves and wonderers
come back to the conker tree.

The Snow Dance

for Debbie

Here is the new year's blank sheet,

the early snow
no one should walk on

but here I am again,
my two left feet

"

"

opening dialogues with the dead
and, though not one sheep lifts its head,

you say "Go! Go! Go!"

Lisboa Muse

Call out her name.
The street's empty well
may answer back

as you lean on unsteady legs,
as the pavement comes apart
under your feet.

*

Inside the Hot Clube, 'Havana Jam'
spread jazz like it's a disease.
You're sliding down (in your dreams)
to kiss her ripped knees.

Studious men blow smoke rings
and stroke their goatees all night.
Their haloes drift, sometimes cling
or bless the notes in flight.

*

Call out her name...

Another missing piece
from this city's grand decay

freefalls to the ground.

*

And no one whistles like the muse
after the final encore.
You'd swap an ear for her cold eyes
but she wants a whole lot more.

She wants the pianist's missing keys.
She wants the drummer's sweat.
She wants the sax's infinite skies.
She wants the unplayable fret.

*

A note from Camané,
a blade from the Bairro Alto,
a loose tile from the moon

over the Jardim Botânico...

she'll kill you several times
and by any means
before the morning comes.

*

But not till she's led you out to the stars,
to their crumbling facade
and whispered Pessoa, her 'private verse'
a thousand others have heard.

She wants the pianist's missing keys.
She wants the studious beards.
She wants the sax's infinite skies.
She wants the final word.

*

Call out her name...

Call out her name...

her name...

her name...

her name...

A Window on the Sea

That split-second, primeval glance.
Forgive me for even recording it
but, stuck to an office ceiling's
polystyrene tile, all year,
a strand of tinsel reminds me
that, beyond the telescopic view,
where concrete gives way to sky,
there has to be sea.

My screen-saver's Cardigan Bay.
I type then stare at cumuli,
print them out in waves.
Perhaps I am the tide.
My chest rises and falls.
There's salt on my breath.
Wind your way down to me.
Pitch your psychedelic towel
and let me stroke your feet.
Drift out to sleep
in that weightless hour
between one and two
when even chief executives dream.

Already I'm half way up the beach,
setting pools in the dips of you,
exploring every cove of you –
your waterbed, your pleasure boat
where concrete gives way to sky
and fixed grins relax in heaps.

No more whip-rounds, innuendoes,
paper knives in the back...
No more waiting twelve months
for the tinsel in your hair.
Just listen to that shell on your desk
calling you to the sea.

Resting with Arbel

She is sculpting a giant ear
out of the plants in her yard,
out of summer's broken promise,
out of scattered earthenware.

Stoned in her wicker chair
I'm grinning that bumpkin grin
she's speared with a pin
to the back of the kitchen door.

Love's just a trick of the light.
I lift the teapot in the glass
and pour it into a bird-bath.

She's on her own again.
Auditions come and go
like speech followed by silence
on the answerphone, like cousins
who visit then disappear.

She raises her Beaujolais
then gets back to the mould.

The cry of a young child
falls, relentlessly,
out of her slice of sky.

It slips through her open arms
but the ear has caught it,
taped it, for posterity.

I lean forward, touch the pane,
wonder if the blood between us
is thin enough by now
for each to see the other's heart.

Queen Canute

Glass water, stone sky.

As if it's her right
she opens my book
and dusts off a page

as a mother might
a son's collar
or the breeze a sail.

Then she steps outside
to inhale, deeply,
before she decides

if it's glass or stone,
this feeling inside

and whether or not
to accept it, the tide.

Nocturne

"Cloudless day,
Night, and a cloudless day; ..."

Robert Graves – 'Counting The Beats'

White masts, metronomes
on the night's high tide,
keep us in time,

our page turner's love.
They tock and chime
as we count the waves.

Mesmerized we slip
between the staves,
lip to lip –

the land and the sea,
making it up,
the same symphony

from the first note
that left this quay
to the last coda

until there's only your ring
(and the lines we cast)
its chime on the railing

to the bells on the masts

now answering

II

i.m. Ann Walters Henry, soprano
1928-2001

Twelve

I was twelve when I murdered for silence.
The senile hero from number nine
trained me to shoot straight.

Silence played a deeper tune
than my father's violin,
its bullets swifter and cleaner
than any note his dusty bow could fire.

So I shot this thrush in its hedge,
allowing it one last song –
the lullaby my mother sang,
my sister's piccolo in flight...

before silencing it
and something else, forever.

I watched it fall through its cage,
the instinct to sing
still alive in its wings,

then listened again.

            A sea wind
bowed the field of reeds beyond.

The Indoor Tune

"Lifelong to be
Seemed the fair colour of the time;"
Thomas Hardy – 'The Musical Box'

Impatient for the light,
her voice, some other sound
besides the indoor tune,
he pushed...

　　　　　The lid gave.

"Love is my reason..." she sang.

Through the bay window
the sun was ironing the sea.

𝄞

Blasé with sopranos,
he sometimes plugged his ears
and closed his eyes.

𝄞

The room grew smaller,
the very house, its musical box.

She sang, he listened,
his big, clumsy hands
cradling cupfuls of tears.

𝄞

He watched as the music unwound
to an indiscernable breath.

The nurse cut a lock of her hair –
so many fair days
he could not see for the glare.

He found a brown envelope,
sealed them inside.

The Broadcast

"Lovely hands. She had such lovely hands,"
my father says, pressing one to his cheek.
"Musician's hands," I'd add, if I could speak.
The blood-seep pales them; peacemaker's hands,
hands that nursed, that danced in air when she sang.

Her voice could make a flower from a fist
and once, whole bouquets of hands at rest
tuned in, across the waves, to hear her sing –
coal hands, steel hands, stone hands... see them bloom
in the bookish laps of post-war living rooms;
hands that knit the tune, hands on a glass,
hands that map remorse, or stifle a kiss...

and my mother's "lovely" hands, after the rain
has finished its applause, dancing again.

The Wardrobe

this faded blue that bled in the rain...
this red that slid too easily from its frame...
this green that danced about her bulge in Spring...

parties, funerals, roses
underneath grey skies, creased seas
beyond the flatlands (where someone
and no one lived and died) rainbows
that fell out of fashion and then came back...

this gown that nearly fell apart...
this silk they had to cut
to reach her heart...

this chill, this breath of air
she wore, that wakes the bones
behind the door...

Black

In a blaze of sealight her old friends
are kissing me on the chapel steps –

Tina Sardinia, Martin Coffee,
Heather, Siân, Edana, Betty...

Custodians of her love
I know them only by their eyes.

𝄞

My cousin's a lady now.
She won't use the tŷ bach.
She brings the gravedigger sweet tea
then lights up on a hard chair
on the patio where Llew,
the neighbour's Tom,
brushes against her legs.

Black suits her.

My cousin keeps me in smoke, tea
and the colour black.

Quartet with Sunlight

oboe

In the absence of cellos
God prescribes an oboe
for my sister's melancholia.

She takes to it, as to a pet
or a fairy tale, nurses it
from a duck to a swan.

It mourns the mauve sunset
from the school cruise
which sets on her wall

and which, in a wing's beat,
will set on her womanhood.

soprano

On tiptoes, a small boy
with enormous chopsticks
feeds the spinner heavy clothes.
Her silks noodle free and fall.

Through blinds, a bar of light
as Madame Butterfly starts to sing
to her new washing machine.

Before the lid is shut,
before the spin,
a rubber web, his tears
go in.

first violin

"Again-again!"
The study smells of corduroy
and resin. "Again!"

His frown is EGBDF
before the notes. "Last time."

It sounds like two violins,
not one.

He's "creased".
It's wrapped in silk

and put to bed.

piano

An open window, a piano lid
cocked, with the sun in it.
In a drafty hall wild Mamgu
kneads the keys.

Net curtains rise
and cover her face, fall
rise...   and cover her face...

unveil the bread of heaven's bride
and cover her face.

Outside
two children play in a mews
the sun has sliced in two.

𝄞

coda

Quack-quack – the smallest windows
Tra-la – must have their right
Squeak-squeak – to scales, arpeggios
Plink-plink – a certain light –

the sort that sticks to kitchen tiles
after the sun has set,
the sort that frowns before it smiles
and gets its ankles wet,

the sort that plays a chord on glass,
that plucks a web in the breeze,
that modulates all we miss
back to its shining key.

Last Call

It was late.
Backstage of the curtains
a car pulled up.

Then someone tired
rose up the steps,
paused at the door.

And inside that moment,
where raised hands wait
for first notes to be played

he saw her standing
in her concert dress,
in the fine, lamplit rain

before the same, deathly steps
diminished
into the night again.

&

Sleep's her auditorium now,
sleep, where sheet music
deafens with her voice.

The seats fill. He fights to stay awake.

The lights go down.

               In the foyer
a stubborn boy crouches
with a pillow to each ear,

an angel counts the takings.

Cuttings

From *The BBC Year Book*, 1950:
'The Girls In Harmony' rehearse another number...

All that counts, in time, is the song
though the rose in your hair suggests
you knew the camera was coming.

Full figures, full-fat smiles,
(no diets or fitness therapy
for Wales's original Spice Girls).

Here was the light stuff that paid –
"A Nightingale Sang in Berkley Square",
"O! Na Byddai'n Haf o Hyd"....

The light stuff that still hurts
at night, when your scrapbook rests
its wings on his heart.

Verse

Lined up, all ages, wall-to-wall,
these stone greetings cards
are not for sale but keen to catch
the last post for words.

I'm hunting a broken angel
who sang me a lullaby
under the dark spires of yews,
under the blinding sky:

She's more to me than Welsh slate
or Scandinavian stone.
She's more to me than flesh and blood.
She's more to me than bone.

I'm hunting the one who planted
this nursery rhyme in my head,
the twinkle-twinkle little stars
that blossom over the dead.

She's past the war graves, past the saints
and past the floral bears,
past the crooked ones like teeth
and past the faded prayers

of those who loved the nursery's
iambic rocking horse
and rode it here, one last time
in a sentimental verse:

She's more to me than Welsh slate
or Scandinavian stone.
She's more to me than flesh and blood.
She's more to me than bone.

Talking Ghosts

My father's talking ghosts, and poltergeists.
When he gesticulates his wedding ring
flies off.

       The blood drains from his face
into his half-ironed shirt.

             He's dressed
the bony music stand with one of her songs,
shaded the *Steinway's* leg from the window's glare.

Diminished to their labels, three bars
of *Cussons Imperial Leather* swim in the sink.

Everything in the bungalow has shrunk

except for the silence, and the goldfish
who mime the same aria, hour by hour,
and grow in exact proportion to their tank.

He's on to reincarnation now, and mediums
whose fishbowls teem with lies.

                Only the sun
haunts, drifting across the mantelpiece,
the variations of her smile,

finding his ring on the floor again.

Maeshendre

A rush of small soles on the pavement
passes and is gone.
A bustle of wings takes off.

Marine Terrace

Here's anywhere now, another life.
It hangs by the hinges of wings

or swims in the sea's terraces
beneath the surface of our days.

Inside *The Cabin*, a new breath blows
the surf from the cappuccinos

and where the stonemason's was
Westcoast Tattoo's moved in

so we grieve them by this rose
on a thigh, this buttock's butterfly,

our town's unfashionable dead.

𝄞

Sometimes, when it's calm enough
to row out into the bay and drift

we can hear the wreck of a *Bechstein* –
Miss Puw, LRCM

playing duets again, with her tail
or teaching Scott Joplin to those

whose fingers slipped between the scales.

Her doorbell holds its pitch then sinks
like a wish into the vestibule.

Behind frayed nets, watching us still,
a shoal of startled eyes.

Acknowledgements

Some of these poems, or versions of them, first appeared in the following publications:

Boomerang, The Literary Review (New Jersey), *Metre, New Welsh Review, Plamak, Planet, Poetry Ireland Review, Poetry Wales, Roundyhouse, Slope, Thumbscrew, The Times Literary Supplement, York Vision* (York University).

'Boys' was first published in the Seren anthology, *Oxygen* (ed. Grahame Davies and Amy Wack). The title poem appeared in *Wading Through Deep Water – The Parkinson's Anthology* (ed. Val Bowden and Tony Curtis).

'Sheds' featured in the BBC2 series *Common Ground*, 'The Slipped Leash' in *A Sense of Place* (BBC Radio Wales).

'Verse' was written for the BBC Wales/Fulmar TV production, *Poets: Can They Hack It?*, in which the author swapped places with a greetings card writer.

'The Broadcast' was commissioned by *Double Yellow* (BBC2 Wales), for National Poetry Day.